A Deck Of Cards

EILEEN DISTASIO-CLARK

With Great Love and Appreciation to those who Have and Do Bless My Life

My Family:

Joseph DeStasio Sr. & Miriam Lucille Baragone DeStasio, My Late Parents.

Andrea Jean DeStasio McIntosh, My Older Sister and their Family.

Joseph DeStasio Jr., My Younger and Only Brother and their Family.

Donna Marie DeStasio Wagner, My Younger Sister and their Family.

My Children:

Eileen, Rebekah, Rachel, S. Michael,

Jennifer, Sharon, Tara, Stephanie,

Apryll, Mikaelah, & M. Trevor

and THEIR Families!!

ACKNOWLEDGEMENTS

First and foremost, I express, deeply, my sincere gratitude to our Heavenly Father for blessing me with the gift and talent of writing! I know I could not do what I do without His assistance.

I also want to acknowledge and express gratitude to the members of my birth family—Joseph Sr., Miriam, Andrea, Joseph Junior, and Donna. All the experiences of my childhood years, experiences that taught me so very much and enabled me to reveal my true self to myself, came about through my experiences and relationships with them.

And, of course, it goes without saying, but I will say it anyway: I also want to acknowledge and note my gratitude to my children, Eileen, Rebekah, Rachel, S. Michael, Jennifer, Sharon, Tara, Stephanie, Apryll, Mikaelah, and M. Trevor, and their families! Through multiple things they said to me, over multiple years, I finally came to the realization that Heavenly Father gave me the gift of writing and opened the doors to these experiences because He knew that by sharing them with others, others could feel His love too.

And He definitely wants us all to know that He, Heavenly Father, Heavenly Mother, and Jehovah truly do loves us!!!

INTRODUCTION

There are sixteen books in this series, which I refer to as *"The Ellie Series."* All of the characters in these stories portray real people from my life. The main characters depict the members of my family: Daddy is my daddy; Mommy is my mommy; Jeannie is my older sister; Junior is my brother; Maria is my younger sister; and Ellie is me. Now, those are not our actual first names, but they do reference us.

The first story in the series presents our Heavenly Father's Plan of Salvation and takes place in the Pre-Earth World. Now, of course, because we all—when we were born—received what is known as The Veil of Forgetfulness, I do not actually remember everything from or about the Pre-Earth World, but I do know about and understand it from much study and worship as a member of The Church of Jesus Christ of Latter-Day Saints, and memories restored to me through the Holy Spirit. So, from this story there is much truth to be learned.

The last story in the series is set in the Post-Mortal World, and presents a depiction of what happens to us after this life. Again, because I have not gone there yet, I cannot say I 'remember' this. But, I have also learned about the Post-Mortal World from much study and worship as a member of The Church of Jesus Christ of Latter-Day Saints.

All of the other stories are based on true events from my life; events that actually occurred when and how they are depicted in these stories. I chose these events because they are among the many occurrences in my life that presented, or revealed that which I already knew without having to be taught, Principles of Eternal Truths.

Also, I chose these events as the settings for my stories because they depict wonderful learning moments from my childhood and adolescent years, lessons that have blessed and benefited me throughout the whole of my life and will forever continue to do so. Also, through these great truths and their consequences in my life, I have been able to share them with many others, whose lives have also been blessed by them.

So, please read and enjoy, then care and share the messages and stories with others!!

Now, there are also a couple of things you can look for:

In each story, the title of the previous story is presented in *italicized* form, the title of the next story is presented in *Capitalized Italicized* form, and the title of the story being read is presented in **emboldened** form.

Also, every story has at least one word that is uncommon or 'created.'

So, as you read, search, find, and have fun!

A DECK OF CARDS

It was another night at Nonna's.

***Uhhh... **Quick Side Note Here:** Nonna is not a name. Well, I guess it could be used as a name, but really, Nonna is not a name. It is a title. It is the Italian word for Grandmother. Since Ellie's family, both sides, were Italian.

Ummmm... **A Side Note to the Side Note:** All four of Ellie's grandparents actually immigrated to America from Italy, so the Stations (Ellie's family) were truly full Italian. Now, of course, since they were all born in America, not just Jeannie, Ellie, Junior, and Maria, but Daddy and Mommy too, they were also American.

Now, back to the Side Note. Being Italian-American, when the family was together, both the Italian and American (aka English) languages were spoken. So, naturally, Grandma was called Nonna and Grandpa was called Nonno. Oh! By the way, that is the Italian word for Grandfather, and it sure did fit Grandpa Rabgaeno. More than anyone else, he was always heard saying "No! No!" to someone. Now, back to the other side.***

As I said, it was another night at Nonna's, that is Nonna Rabgaeno, Mommy's mom, and as all nights at Nonna's went. Well almost all nights, all the kids got together and played downstairs in the cellar, while the grown-ups sat at the dining room table talking and playing card games.

***Uhhh... **Another Side-Note:** The younger cousins, and some of the older cousins, always wanted to play in the cellar. Now, the older cousins, well, at least a few of them, did not enjoy playing in the cellar like they did when they were younger because, to them, that was just 'kid's stuff' and, of course, they did not consider themselves kids anymore. So, most of the time, they just watched T.V. or played games upstairs, where the bedrooms were.

But there were those of the not-so-older cousins who did like to play in the cellar because they really enjoyed taking care of and playing with their younger cousins. That actually made them happy because they really did like doing things that would make others happy.

Okay, so now that you understand all of that. I hope you do, we will go back to the other side.***

It was pretty early when the Stations arrived at Nonna's house. Most of the other family members that were already there were grown-ups, and there were enough of them there for them to begin playing their card games. However, none of the little kids were there yet, and Ellie really did not want to play upstairs with the older kids, she thought the stuff they liked to play was boring. So she just sat with Daddy and watched the grown-ups play one round each of Rummy, Gin-Rummy, and Bridge. Even though Ellie did not really play the card games with them, to her, they looked kind of boring too, she did shuffle the cards for them and, of course, she loved being with Daddy.

About the time they were ready to begin playing Poker, the rest of the families arrived and, of course, Ellie was very happy to take the little cousins down to the cellar. Now, she was not the only one who wanted to play with them; so did Jennie, Junior, Marie, Tricia, and Ebbie, and once down there, they played lots and lots, and lo... well you get the idea; they played lots of games!

First, they played Hide-and-Seek, until Ellie got stuck behind the furnace. Being as small as she was, even at sixteen, that was not something that seemed like it could have been possible. But for Ellie, even the impossible was possible because, somehow, in some way, she always managed to do *some pretty crazy things.* How she did that no one ever really could explain, even Ellie, but somehow, she did. And that night, one of those crazy things was getting stuck behind the furnace. She tried to walk out from behind the furnace, but that did not work. She tried holding onto the furnace—which by the way, was not in use because it was summertime—to pull herself out from behind it, but that did not work either.

"My head is stuck," she cried out quietly and, because she did not want to scare the little cousins, she did so in a joking kind of voice, but Jeannie could see that it was not a joke. When it was quite clear to everyone else that she could not get herself out from behind the furnace, Jeannie ran upstairs to get help.

"Hey," she shouted, "we need help! Ellie is stuck behind the furnace!"

"What?" came the not-so-surprised reply from everyone at the table.

"How did she get stuck behind the furnace?" Daddy asked, with a 'not again' vocal tone, as he got up to go down and 'rescue' Ellie.

"I don't know," Jeannie replied, "but somehow she did."

Once down in the cellar, Daddy made his way around all the toys that were on the floor and across the room to where the furnace was. Truly, he could see that there was very little room between the furnace and the wall, but he could also see that the lack of space was not what caused Ellie's entrapment. It did not take more than a glance for him to see that somehow, she had gotten her ponytail entangled in some wires that were hanging down from the ceiling behind the furnace. Teasingly, and it was teasingly, because he knew and appreciated how much Ellie loved long hair, and he did too, he said, "Well, Ellie, it looks like I just might have to cut off your ponytail."

With great alarm, and a volume no one would ever have believed could come from Ellie—she was a very soft-spoken person—she cried, "NO! NO!! NO!!! DO NOT CUT MY HAIR!!!!"

With a little chuckle in his voice, Daddy then said, "Okay, Ellie, I will not cut your hair, but you have to stay very still so I can get it untangled from the wires."

Now, still was not a skill that Ellie possessed. Remember, she was always moving, ALWAYS! But somehow, as evidence of how important her hair was to her, she did manage to stay still enough, long enough for Daddy to untangle her ponytail from the wires and pull Ellie out from behind the furnace.

Before Daddy went back upstairs, Ellie gave him a great big, 'little hug' and said thank you, over and over and over and ov... well you get the idea. She could not have been more grateful for anything than she was for Daddy saving her hair. Now, crazy as that might sound, it was true! As I said, Ellie loves long hair. She actually, truly, always wanted her hair to grow all the way down to her feet when she was standing up, but sadly, that never happened. It seemed the longest Ellie's hair ever grew was just halfway down her back, that is halfway between her shoulders and her waist.

Nonetheless, Ellie was happy to have her hair that long since it could not grow any longer.

Now, after Daddy went back upstairs, and the kids were ready to resume their play, Jeannie suggested that they play a different game. So, after numerous suggestions were made, they all agreed to play Finders Keepers.

Third Side Note:** Finders Keepers was what some kids back then—which was quite a while ago—remember Ellie was a little girl, a not-so-little girl, and a teenage girl quite some time ago. Anyway, another name for that game is Hidden Object, wherein an object, any type of object like a small ball, or a stone, or a key, or a… well, you know what I am saying, wherein something is hidden by one person while all the other players close their eyes and hide their faces so they do not see where the object is being hidden. Then, when the object is hidden, everyone except the person who hid the hidden object, searches for it. Whoever finds it, is the next one to hide it. Now, back to the other side.

All was going well, for a while, but then…

"Oh no!" Junior cried a little dramatically, while running up the steps, "Ellie is stuck!"

"What?" came the reply from everyone at the table, again with a 'not again' tone.

"She got her foot stuck in that hole in the floor," Junior explained.

"Oh, no," Mommy sighed as she got up from the table and followed Junior down to the cellar, where indeed she saw Ellie standing in the middle of the room with her foot stuck in the hole, which was a drain to the sewer.

"How did you manage to do this?" Mommy asked as she pulled, carefully and gently, Ellie's foot out of the drain opening.

"We are playing Finders Keepers, and I was looking for the tennis ball that Tricia hid," Ellie explained. "I guess I was looking so hard for the ball that I was not looking at where I was walking."

"Well," Mommy replied, "at least it does not look like you injured your foot. How does it feel?"

"It hurts a little, but it is okay," Ellie replied.

"Good," Mommy said as she tuned in and headed for the stairs. She then added, "Now, I think you should play something else.

'But what?' they all wondered. Every time someone suggested a game, someone else expressed a lack of interest in it. Since they all wanted to play together, they kept trying to think of something they would all like to play. Now, some of the older cousins, who were done playing games, went upstairs to watch television, but the rest of them decided, using the chalk they found in one of the toy baskets, to draw a Hop-Scotch on the floor and play that.

Even though the heel of a shoe is typically what one uses to play Hop-Scotch, since they could not find any of those, they all chose different things to toss into the squares and then retrieve. After playing Hop-Scotch for... hmmm... I do not know how long they played that, but after they were done, thinking it should soon be time to go home, they put away all the toys that they had gotten out and went upstairs. And, pretty soon, they all did hear their parents say, "Okay, kids, it is now time to go home." And that was what they all did.

Now, that was how almost every family get-together at Nonna Rabgaeno's went, the little kids, with a few of the not-so-older kids, played games in the cellar while the older kids played. Whatever it was, they played upstairs in the bedrooms, and the grown-ups played cards in the dining room. Everyone seemed to enjoy it; no one ever really complained. Oh sure, there were times when disputes burst out, but they were never really serious and they were always resolved quickly. But sometimes, the kids, even the little cousins, did not want to play in the cellar. So, more and more often, they just stayed upstairs and watched television. Well, Ellie did not do that. Or they went for a walk around the neighborhood, Ellie definitely did that. Or they sat on the patio and talked about this, that, and everything else they could think of.

But one evening, after taking several walks, sitting on the patio and talking about everything they could think of to talk about, knowing that their parents were not done playing cards, and after multiple whiney expressions of *What Next*, Ellie suggested that they play cards.

"Yeah, why don't we?" they all agreed. But where would they get **a deck of cards**? None of them had cards of their own, and they were pretty sure their parents only had the deck they were playing with. Still, they wanted to give it a try, so they went to their parents and asked them if they— their parents—had any extra decks of cards that they—the kids—could play with.

To their—the kids'—surprise, they—the grown— did have an extra deck. In fact, they had several extra decks. Apparently, some of the grown-ups always brought **a deck of cards** with them, just in case no one else brought **a deck of cards.**

Well, that made the kids very happy because now, they had something different to do. With a deck in hand, Ellie led the way to the living room, where they all sat down on the floor in a circle to play cards. But which game would they play? Go Fish? Slap Jack? Match Game?

Now, when Ellie suggested Match Game, everyone else, in unison and with strong emotion, quickly shouted, "No!" They were absolutely certain that if they played that game, because Ellie's memory was way too good, no one would have even the slightest of chances at getting any matches, much less winning.

So, they bantered back and forth, and forth and back, and back and fo... well, you know what they did; they disputed over Go Fish and Slap Jack, until they finally came to an agreement. They would play Go Fish.

And they did, at least three times, with someone different winning each time! But, when they were done 'fishing,' and they could see that their parents were still not done playing whichever card game they were playing. The kids decided to play another game and that was Slap Jack.

Now, all the girls knew that they had to be pretty fast at slapping Jack, because if the boys slapped them—well, their hands—when they were slapping Jack, it would really hurt. According to all the girls, the boys just did not know what it meant to be gentle. In fact, that was why they had chosen to play Go Fish instead of Slap Jack. But, now, because they had already 'gone fishing' and they still did not want to play the Match Game with Ellie, but they did still want Ellie to play with them, they decided Slap Jack is what they would play. And they did, about six times!! Oh, and of course, throughout each game, dozens of very vocalized "Ow! That hurt!" screams were heard by everyone. Absolutely everyone by in the house, in the neighborhood, in the city, in the state, in... well, okay, I think I am going a little overboard. But it was quite clear that the girls had been right about the boys. And it had been just as clear that the girls could not move their hands away from Jack fast enough.

Now, by the time the kids were done playing Slap Jack, the grown-ups were also done playing whichever card game they had been playing. So, everyone put away their cards, got their stuff, and headed out to their cars to go home. Well, at least those who came by car; there was one family who just had to walk up the street. Now, as they all departed, there seemed to be a different feeling than there usually was, when leaving Nonna's house. Ellie could feel it, but she did not understand it.

Once home, because it was rather late, Jeannie, Ellie, Junior, and Maria got ready for bed while Mommy got ready to watch T.V. and Daddy got ready to relax in his comfy, overstuffed easy chair and read the newspaper. After baths were done, teeth were brushed, and good-nights were said, the four Stations kids said their prayers and hopped into bed.

It did not take long for Jeannie, Junior, or Maria to fall asleep, they were quite worn out. But Ellie? Well, she too was tired, but she could not fall asleep. Of course, you must recall that sleep is not something Ellie ever did well; but this night, it was the thoughts and questions dancing around in her mind that were keeping her from drifting off into Dreamland.

'What were those thoughts and questions,' you may be wondering. Well, I will tell you. Ellie had enjoyed playing Go Fish; it was a fun game. But she did not enjoy seeing some of her cousins do things that, at least in her mind, amounted to cheating. To her cousins and maybe to everyone else, they were just game tactics and were perfectly acceptable. But Ellie could not accept them. She knew that games—all games—had rules and that the rules were expected to be followed. She understood that it was not okay to break the rules and it was not okay to make up your own rules.

As she pondered that, many of the things she had learned in Catechism and many of the things she had talked about with Daddy and Mommy, came to her mind. It was very obvious, even from the Bible, itself, that God wants us to be honest, and good, and 'play by the rules.' That was why He gave us—among other things, many other things—The Ten Commandments, which Ellie spent the rest of the time that she was awake thinking about. And these were her thoughts.

'God told us, in the First Commandment that He gave to us, "Thou shalt have no other gods before me." So, He wants us to do everything that we do in ways that will please and honor Him. That is fair, because He is the one who gives us everything we have, and what He gives us is always good! So, that means we should always, in all ways, play by the rules, especially His rules.'

Ellie paused her thoughts for few moments, thinking a little deeper about that. To her—and she believes to everyone—that had to make a lot of sense because she knew and believes that everyone else has to know that no one could know as well as God knows what is right and best for us, for all of us!!

As she laid quietly, pondering, she thought, 'In His Second Commandment, He told us, "Thou shalt not make unto thee any graven image."'

***Uhhh... let me step in with a little bit of a **Fourth Side Note:** At the time Ellie was thinking these thoughts, a long time ago, she did not really fully understand what this one meant. She knew that there is only One True God for all of us, so she did understand that it is not okay to worship anyone or anything else, or to worship God in a way that He did not design.

What she did not understand then, but she came to understand later, was that making things, anything like work, entertainment, money, material possessions, popularity... anything, more important to us than giving our time to God and obeying His laws, is the same thing as idolatry. Now, back to the other side.***

'So, I know that God is the only one from whom we must 'take orders,' and that too means we must play by the rules!

'His Third Commandment' she pondered, 'tells us, "Thou shalt not take the name of the Lord thy God in vain." That one is super easy to understand. No one should ever swear, especially using His name to do it. In fact, no one should ever use bad language at all. He does not talk like that, so we must not talk like that. That is His rule too!

'His Fourth Commandment reminds us to "Remember the sabbath day, to keep it holy." That is another easy one. The only thing we should be doing on Sunday, if we are going to be playing by His rules, is stuff like going to church, His church, studying the scriptures, praying... stuff that Jesus would do. And Jesus always played by God's rules.

'The Fifth Commandment reminds us to "Honour thy father and thy mother." So, from that I understand this. As kids, we are supposed to...' Ellie thought a little more deeply, then, 'No! Not just supposed to, we must love and respect our parents. But I do not believe that we are only to love and respect them when we are kids. We are to do that always and they are to do the same for their parents. There is no limit. So, that is just another way we are expected, always to play by His rules.

'Now, let me think... what is the Sixth Commandment? Oh yeah! I remember!! And that is definitely very obvious when it comes to reminding us that we must play by God's rules. It tells us, "Thou shalt not kill." That is a rule that should never, by anyone, even be considered to be disobeyed. Of course, I guess... there might be times like war or self-defense. But I am absolutely certain that, if there were to be a good and acceptable reason for that, He will let us know!

'Now the Seventh Commandment, "Thou shalt not commit adultery." Yep! Like all the other commandments that is a very strong reminder that we MUST obey God's rules and live moral lives, clean and pure!

'His Eighth Commandment, "Thou shalt not steal," orders us to never take anything from anyone. In fact, we must never take anything that does not belong to us, from anywhere. And if we do, we are not playing by God's rules; we are breaking them.

'He tells us in the Ninth Commandment, "Thou shalt not bear false witness against thy neighbor." That is another rule that lets us know that we must be completely honest in every way, on every day, about everything! And if we are not, we are breaking His rules!

'And the Tenth Commandment, "Thou shalt not covet." Hmmm... covet? That means... It means to want something really badly. But... oh, wait a minute. He says we shall not covet thy neighbors' stuff. Okay, so that lets us know that we cannot envy what others have or try to take what is not ours! If we do, we are breaking God's rules. And, it will only bring us unhappiness and dissatisfaction.'

"Yes!" Ellie said softly, but with full confidence and commitment, "It is never okay to break the rules, especially God's rules, but any other rules too, and it is not okay to make up our own rules to replace rules that have already been made by those who have the responsibility and authority to make them, whether they apply to a game, a program, society, anything!"

As Ellie finally relaxed and began to wonder off into dreamland, she did so with a deep and sincere commitment to always play... no, not just play, to always live, in all ways, on all days, by the rules! And that was something Ellie always held fast to playing by the rules, whether they were God's rules, rules to a game, rules called laws, rules... well I am certain you know exactly what I am saying; Ellie was just not one to defy or break the rules. When she learned them, she followed them, in all ways on all days! In fact, she wrote the Ten Commandments on **a deck of cards,** and carried them with her so as to never forget to play by His rules.

ABOUT THE AUTHOR

Eileen DiStasio-Clark is the second oldest of four children. She is the mother of eleven children and grandmother to twenty-three grandchildren, to date. As a member of The Church of Jesus Christ of Latter-Day Saints, she serves in various positions, teaching, leading, and ministering to children, youth, and adults. Currently, she is also a Family History Missionary. Eileen established the Pursuit of Excellence Institute of Family Education, a non-profit organization focused on strengthening the family. Presently she holds an A.A., a B.A., and an M.A. in Clinical Psychology and is working on the completion of her Doctoral Degree.

www.ingramcontent.com/pod-product-compliance
Lightning Source LLC
Chambersburg PA
CBHW051251120626
46547CB00014B/1901